NATURE FILES

NATURE FILES – ANIMAL COMMUNICATION
was produced by

David West 👥 **Children's Books**
7 Princeton Court
55 Felsham Road
London SW15 1AZ

Designer: Julie Joubinaux
Editor: Gail Bushnell
Picture Research: Carlotta Cooper

First published in Great Britain by Heinemann
Library, Halley Court, Jordan Hill, Oxford
OX2 8EJ, part of Harcourt Education.
Heinemann is a registered trademark
of Harcourt Education Ltd.

07 06 05 04 03
10 9 8 7 6 5 4 3 2 1

ISBN 0 431 18241 8 (HB)
ISBN 0 431 18248 5 (PB)

British Library Cataloguing in Publication Data

Ganeri, Anita, 1961-
Animal communication. - (Nature Files)
1. Animal communication - Juvenile literature
I. Title
591.5'9

Printed and bound in Italy

PHOTO CREDITS :
Abbreviations: t-top, m-middle, b-bottom, r-right,
l-left, c-centre.

Front cover - all Corbis Images. Pages 3 & 9bl, 5t &
28–29 (Phil Savoie), 4–5 (Elio Della Ferrera), 6t,
21m, 27t (John Cancalosi), 6b, 25b (Anup Shah), 7
9tr (Jose B. Ruiz), 8–9 (Bruce Davidson), 9tl (Colin
Seddon), 9br (Jurgen Freund), 11t (Doc White), 11
20b (Ingo Arndt), 12r (Bjorn Forsberg), 13tl (Lynn
Stone), 13tr (David Tipling), 13b, 24br (John
Downer), 14tr (Hans Christoph Kappel), 14br, 15b
(Todd Pusser), 15t, 21t (Dietmar Nill), 15m (Artur
Tabor), 16b, 18l, 28b (Peter Oxford), 17t, 29t (Jeff
Foott), 17b (Tom Vezo), 19b (Georgette Douwma),
21br (Geoff Dore), 21bm (Naturbild), 22t (Andrew
Cooper), 23m (David Shale), 26bl (Steven D. Miller
27b (Neil Bromhall), 28t (Brian Lightfoot), 29b (Da
Watts) - naturepl.com. 4t & 10t (David McNew), 1
(Peter Weimann), 19t, 26t (Norbert Wu) - Still
Pictures. 5b & 22b (Satoshi Kuribayashi), 12l (Rob
Bush), 14tr (Friedemann Koster/SAL), 16t (Bill
Paton/SAL), 23t (Ralph A. Lewin), 24l - Oxford
Scientific Films. 17m, 18r, 20t - Corbis Images. 19m
(Scott Tuason), 21bl (Roger Steene), 23b (Peter
Herring), 26br (Jim Greenfield) - Image Quest 3D.

Every effort has been made to contact copyright
holders of any material reproduced in this book. An
omissions will be rectified in subsequent printings if
notice is given to the publishers.

*An explanation of difficult words can be
found in the glossary on page 31.*

NATURE FILES

ANIMAL COMMUNICATION

Anita Ganeri

Heinemann
LIBRARY

CONTENTS

Every morning and evening, group of howler monkeys sing in chorus to warn enemies away from their rainforest territory. Their voices ca be heard about 8 kilometres away.

INTRODUCTION

Communication means sending and receiving messages. A dog barking, a bird singing, the glow of a firefly or the bright colours of a butterfly – these are all signals which animals use to communicate with each other. These signals enable them to find food, attract a mate, guard their homes, show their feelings and warn off enemies. All of these are vital to an animal's survival. Messages can be sent over long and short distances.

A male bird of paradise uses its plumage to attract a mate. This Count Raggi's bird of paradise hangs upside down in a tree to show off its brilliant tail feathers.

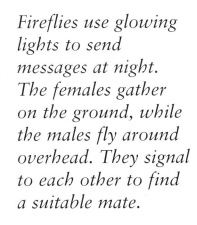

Fireflies use glowing lights to send messages at night. The females gather on the ground, while the males fly around overhead. They signal to each other to find a suitable mate.

Male atlas moths use their feathery antennae to detect smells released by the females. The females give off these scents to attract a mate.

Communication is used by members of the same species to keep in touch with each other, find food and identify a mate. Other messages are designed to keep enemies away.

WARNING SIGNALS

Animals have several ways of warning off enemies. Some use bright colours to inform predators that they are unpleasant to eat (see pages 20–21). Others let out loud roars, calls and screams or use threatening faces and postures when they are under attack.

If another animal comes too close, a rattlesnake shakes the rattle of loose scales at the end of its tail. Usually this warns an enemy away.

A cheetah cub has a thick mane of hair along its back. This makes the cub look bigger than it actually is, so that would-be attackers keep their distance.

SIGHT, SOUND AND SMELL

Many animal signals involve the three senses of sight, sound and smell. The type of communication an animal uses depends on where it lives and how far the information has to travel. Visual signals are good over short distances. But loud sounds can travel further, especially through water and thick forest. Smells can spread far and wide on the breeze and last for several hours or days.

Children learn to write at school.

ELECTRIC SHOCK

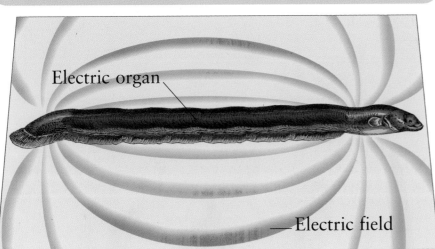

Electric organ

Electric field

Electric eels from South America have rows of organs along their bodies. The organs produce electrical signals which the eels use for navigation and communication. The eels can turn the pattern of signals on and off, and may use them to identify themselves and attract a mate.

Vervet monkeys use a system of sounds to warn each other of different types of danger. For example, they have different calls for different predators.

SUPER SENSES

Animals receive information through their senses. Depending on how they communicate, some senses are sharper than others. For example, animals with good eyesight use visual signals.

EYES AND EARS

Animals that communicate with sound and colour need good hearing and eyesight. The fennec fox lives in the Sahara Desert. It comes out at night to hunt for food, using its huge ears to listen out for insects and lizards.

A SHARK'S SUPER SENSES

A shark uses special senses to hunt. Cells in its skin can 'taste' the water for prey. Folds of skin on its nose channel water inside. Here sense cells pick up the smell of prey. Cells along its body and sense organs in its head, called Lorenzi flasks, help it to sense vibrations in the water and detect prey.

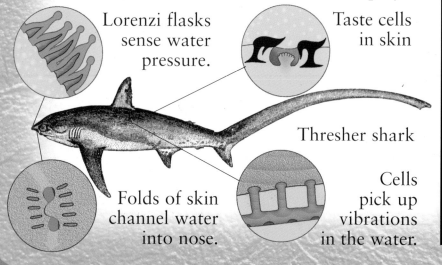

Lorenzi flasks sense water pressure.

Taste cells in skin

Thresher shark

Folds of skin channel water into nose.

Cells pick up vibrations in the water.

Amazing FACT

Dogs have a brilliant sense of smell. A German Shepherd dog has over 40 times more smell cells in its nose than a human being. Its sense of smell is about a million times sharper than ours. Dogs use their sense of smell to find food and a mate, and to identify visitors to their territories.

Police dogs are used to catch criminal

Bushbabies have large eyes that let lots of light in, so that they can see well in the dark, up to 30 metres in starlight.

A snake's forked tongue flicks in and out to pick up smells from the air and ground. It transfers these to pockets lined with sensitive cells in the roof of its mouth.

An insect's large eyes have thousands of tiny lenses for spotting small movements.

TOUCHY FEELY

Some animals have sensitive antennae, hairs and whiskers. Insects used their antennae for touching, smelling and tasting. The touch-sensitive 'hairs' on an insect's body are also important. They can detect vibrations in the air and sense if another creature is approaching.

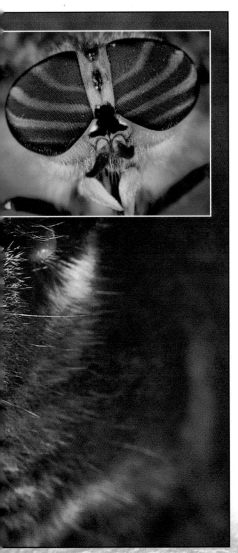

A catfish's whiskers are sensitive to touch and taste. The fish uses them to search out its prey in the muddy water where it lives, and decides if it is worth eating.

Many types of animal use calls, roars and chirps to send messages to each other. Sound travels long distances through air and water.

WOLF CHORUS

Wolves live in family groups, called packs. They use scent markings and sounds to mark out and defend their territory. The wolves' famous long, deep, mournful howl helps to advertise the pack's presence and keep any rival packs away.

When one member of a wolf pack starts to howl, all of the others join in the chorus.

Amazing FACT

Howler monkeys live in the South American rainforests. Sound is a good way of communicating in the tangle of trees. Every day, howler monkeys roar to warn rivals away. Their ear-splitting voices can be heard 8 kilometres away.

A howler monkey in full voice.

Whales appear to use their songs to keep their groups together. Whales have loud but very low voices, that are below the range at which humans can hear.

WHALE OF A SONG

Some whales build up series of sounds into 'songs' which they use for communication. Astonishingly, the songs of humpback whales can be heard hundreds of kilometres away. The songs may last for at least 10 minutes, and as long as half an hour.

CHIRPING BUGS

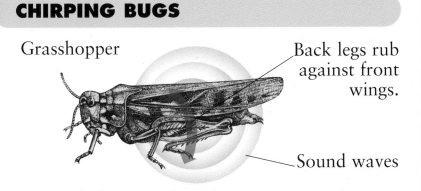

Grasshopper

Back legs rub against front wings.

Sound waves

Male grasshoppers and crickets use songs to attract a mate. They use a special method, called stridulation, to produce chirping sounds. Crickets rub their front wings together. Grasshoppers scrape their back legs against the front wings.

This male natterjack toad inflates his balloon-like vocal sac to amplify or increase his mating call.

11

In spring, when breeding begins, beautiful bird song can be heard everywhere. It is thought that parent birds teach their young to sing.

CALLS AND SONGS

Birds communicate with calls and songs. Calls are made of simple notes, and are used to warn of danger and keep in touch. Songs are more complex and more musical. They are usually sung by male birds, to attract a mate during the breeding season and to defend their nests and territories.

Amazing FACT

Some birds are famous for being able to copy human speech. One of the most talkative birds kept in captivity was an African grey parrot called Prudle. She could say almost 800 words. Budgerigars and mynah birds are also excellent mimics. Some wild birds are able to imitate the sounds of other birds.

Kakapos are nocturnal parrots from New Zealand. Males make loud, booming calls to attract females in the dark. Some years, the birds do not boom and so do not breed.

Each species of bird has its own distinctive song. Male skylarks have a long, tuneful song. They sing as they fly to attract a mate and to warn away rivals.

Grey parrots are popular pets.

KEEPING IN CONTACT

The information contained in an individual bird's call or song can help other birds to identify it. This is particularly important for birds which live and nest in large colonies, such as penguins and sea-birds. Parent penguins leave the colony to find food for their chicks. When they return, they call out to locate their chicks.

On its return to the colony, an adult penguin calls out and waits for a reply. Amazingly, it can pick out its own chick's particular call from among thousands of others.

Migrating birds use contact calls to keep the flock together. Geese cover thousands of kilometres, making honking noises to keep in touch.

Many bats and dolphins hunt at night or in murky water where visual signals are useless. Instead, they rely on sound. They use a system called echolocation to detect food and find their way around.

BAT VOICES

At night, bats leave their roosts to look for food. Insect-eating bats use echolocation to track down their prey. You can read how this works on the next page. Bats use echolocation so accurately that they can locate the tiniest midges in the dark.

Some moths take avoiding action. They detect the bat's calls and clicks before the bat locates them, and quickly fly away.

Oilbirds live in South America.

Amazing FACT

Oilbirds live in dark caves, often as deep as 1 kilometre underground. They spend all day asleep, only leaving the caves at night to forage for fruit in the forest. Inside their caves, they use echolocation like bats to navigate, find their roosting ledges and avoid colliding with other birds.

River dolpins have such poor eyesight that they can only distinguish between light and dark. They use echolocation to find fish, shrimps and squid to eat.

Echolocating bats feed mainly on insects, like moths, which they snatch in mid-air.

ECHOLOCATION

To detect objects in its path, a bat sends out high-pitched calls or clicking sounds. The sounds hit a solid object. From the returning echoes, the bat can tell what the object is and how far away it is.

Sound emitted by bat (purple) —

Echo of sound from moth (white)

Bats, like this long-eared bat, have large, sensitive ears and superb hearing for picking up echoes.

DOLPHIN LANGUAGE

Like bats, many species of dolphin use echolocation. They produce a series of fast, high-pitched sounds through their blowholes or foreheads. Some may even use sound to stun or disorientate their prey. Dolphins also use a wide range of squeaks, clicks, whistles and barks to communicate with each other.

Dolphins are very sociable animals which live in family groups. Scientists think they use different sounds to identify themselves to others and warn them of danger.

SCENTS AND SMELLS

Some animals have an excellent sense of smell and use scents to send and receive messages. Smell is used to attract a mate, warn off enemies and mark out territories.

MOTH PERFUME

Many insects use special chemicals, called pheromones, to communicate. These chemicals are often smells. They are extremely powerful – it takes only a tiny amount to send a strong signal. A female moth releases pheromones into the air to attract a mate.

Deer have scent glands just below their eyes. They rub their faces against the branches of trees to leave scent messages for other members of their herd.

A male moth has feathery antennae to pick up a female moth's pheromones. The antennae are very sensitive and can detect scents from a distance of several kilometres away.

SMELLY TRAILS

Ants live in colonies or groups many thousands strong. Like moths, many ants use pheromones to lay scent trails and send messages to each other. When they find a source of food, they lay a scent trail between it and their nest for other ants to follow. Other species of ant do not use scents, to avoid attracting more aggressive insects.

Ants follow a scent trail to help them find food.

Food source

Incoming ants pick up scent trail.

Ants return to nest by following scent trail.

Amazing FACT

A skunk has a terrible secret weapon. To drive off predators, it first stamps its front feet and lifts up its tail. If this does not work, it does a handstand on its front feet, with its rear in the air, and sprays out a foul-smelling liquid. The dreadful smell can be detected several metres away.

Like rhinos, hippos mark their territories with trails of dung. Hippos use their tails to spread out the dung as they walk along.

SCENT MARKING

Many animals use scent signals to mark out the borders of their territories. These warn would-be intruders to keep well clear. Male cats, such as tigers, mark trees or grass with strong-smelling urine to show where their territories are. Rhinoceroses leave piles of dung around the edges of their territories.

A skunk only sprays if threatened.

17

Sending messages with distinctive patterns and bright colours is called visual communication. This form of communication is very important among animals. But the senders and receivers must have good eyesight.

VISUAL SIGNALS

Visual signals cannot travel far and can be blocked by objects such as trees. But they are useful for sending messages over short distances. Groups of ring-tailed lemurs wander through the forest, looking for food. Each lemur keeps its striped tail raised like a flag.

Amazing FACT

Thousands of fish live on a coral reef and life is very crowded. However it is vital for individual fish to recognise members of their own species so that they can pick out mates and rivals. The bright colours and striking markings of fish, such as butterfly fish, act like identity tags and can also help to confuse predators

A male mandrill has a scarlet and blue coloured face and bottom. These show that the mandrill is strong and powerful

The ring-tailed lemur's raised tail shows the others where it is and keeps the group safely together. Lemurs also wave their tails at rivals to warn them off.

ALL CHANGE

Some animals are able to communicate by changing their colour. Cuttlefish have thousands of tiny pigment sacs in their skins. By expanding or shrinking the sacs, the cuttlefish changes colour. It uses specific patterns to warn off predators, attract a mate or distract its prey.

A shoal of butterfly fish.

By changing the shape of the colour sacs in its skin, a cuttlefish can send ripples of colour and pattern shimmering across its body.

A cleanerfish 'grooming' a moray eel. Cleanerfish have bright stripes so that their clients do not mistake them for prey and eat them.

19

Some animals use bright colours, such as black, red and yellow, as warning signs. They send an instant message to predators that their owners are poisonous or dangerous to eat.

DANGER: KEEP AWAY

Animals that use warning colours include wasps, bees, frogs, snakes and sea slugs. Among the world's deadliest animals are the arrow-poison frogs from South America. Their brilliantly coloured skins contain a lethal poison (below).

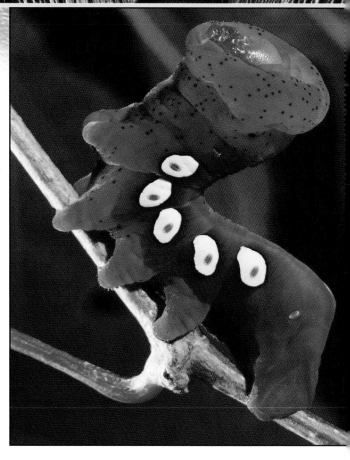

Butterfly and moth caterpillars are open to attacks from hungry birds. Some, like this black swallowtail caterpillar, use warning colours to advertise their terrible taste.

If it gets into the bloodstream, a drop of frog poison can kill a large monkey or even a human. Local people extract the poison and use it to tip their hunting arrows.

FLASHY COLOURS

Some animals use flashes of colours or markings to startle predators. At rest, many moths are well hidden by their dull brown wings. But if threatened, some flash bright markings on their back wings. The markings look like the eyes of a bigger, fiercer creature, and fool predators into leaving the moth alone.

If a bird disturbs them, some grasshoppers fly off, flashing their colourful back wings. Then they land again, fold up their wings and blend into the background.

Amazing FACT

When a blue-ringed octopus is threatened, bright blue rings start to glow all over its body. The rings warn that the octopus has a deadly poisonous bite that can kill in minutes. Fortunately, these tiny octopuses are usually quite timid.

The 'real' coral snake is deadly poisonous. The harmless 'false' coral snake mimics its distinctive stripes for protection.

COLOUR COPIERS

Not all brightly-coloured animals are as dangerous as they seem. All kinds of harmless animals imitate stinging or poisonous animals to trick predators into avoiding them. Hoverflies have yellow and black stripes like wasps or bees, but they are harmless and cannot sting.

A blue-ringed octopus.

Wasp   *Hoverfly*

For some animals that are active at night or live in the dark, light is a good way of sending signals. These creatures can produce their own light, using special chemicals or bacteria inside their bodies.

FIREFLY GLOW

Fireflies, or glow-worms, are small beetles which make yellowish-green lights through chemical reactions inside their bodies. Male and female fireflies flash their lights at each other to attract a mate.

The female common glow-worm cannot fly. She climbs up a grass stalk or twig, waving her glowing tail in the air to attract a mate.

Each species of firefly has its own pattern of flashes so that members of the same species can recognise each other. In the breeding season, males flash their lights on and off in unison.

Amazing FACT

Dinoflagellates are microscopic plants which drift in the ocean. Because of their size, they are usually invisible, but some produce their own light using chemicals inside their bodies. If a wave churns up the sea at night, they make the water sparkle and shine with blue-green light.

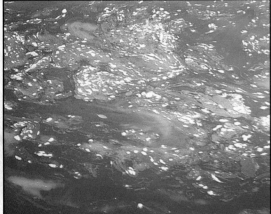

Glowing dinoflagellates.

UNDERWATER LIGHTS

It is pitch black in the depths of the sea because no sunlight can reach that far down. Many deep-sea fish cope with the darkness by making their own lights. They use these lights to identify themselves, attract mates, find food and escape from danger. Flashlight fish (below) have glowing 'headlights' under each eye. These are produced by large organs in their bodies which contain millions of luminous bacteria.

Flashlight fish can turn their lights on and off to confuse predators, and swivel them to search for food.

Lanternfish have rows of light-producing organs dotted along the sides of their bodies.

The way you smile, frown, walk or stand can tell other people a great deal about how you are feeling. Many animals also use facial expressions and body language to communicate with each other.

DANCING BEES

When a honeybee discovers a rich source of food, it returns to its nest or hive and passes on this information by dancing. The length and type of the dance it performs tell the other bees how good the food is and where they can find it.

If a cat feels threatened, it arches its back and raises its fur to make itself look bigger and more frightening. It also hisses and bares its teeth to scare off attackers.

If food is close by, the bee dances in a circle. If it is more than 80 metres away, the bee wags its tail as it dances. Other bees pick up the scent of the flowers it has visited.

A Virginia opossum playing dead.

Amazing FACT

Some animals deliberately send the wrong signals to get themselves out of trouble. If a Virginia opossum is under attack, it collapses, rolls over on its side and pretends to be dead. Many predators then leave it alone. Once the danger is over, the opossum jumps up and runs away.

SENDING SIGNALS

The way in which an animal moves or holds its body can send a wide range of messages, from fear to playfulness to anger. Many animals that feel threatened try to make themselves appear larger, more powerful and more frightening that they actually are. Elephants, for example, trumpet and flap their ears. Swans act in a similar way, by hissing loudly and spreading out their wings.

If a horse is frightened, it holds its ears back and its tail low. An excited horse pricks up its ears and holds its tail up high.

CHIMPS PULLING FACES

Thoughtful   Frightened   Angry

Chimpanzees have expressive faces. They are among the few animals that can use facial expressions to show their feelings. Like human beings, they can pull faces to show happiness, anger or fear. However, a chimp that is grinning and showing its teeth is feeling frightened or insecure, not smiling.

Young chimps push their mouths forward in a pout. They seem to be begging for food.

25

One of the main functions of communication is to find a mate for breeding. Competition among male animals to find a mate is fierce. Many perform courtship displays to attract females.

SHOWING OFF

A male animal has to attract a female's attention so that she picks him out from the crowd. One of the claws of a male fiddler crab is large and brightly coloured. The crab waves it in a particular way to attract a female.

The male fiddler crab waves his claw in circles as he stands on tiptoe, or swings his claw round. He also uses his claw to fight off rivals.

When a male yellowhead jawfish meets a female he begins a courtship dance in which they sway and nod to each other.

Male cuckoo wrasses change colour in the breeding season, so that females can identify which males are ready to mate. Females are drably coloured.

SONG AND DANCE

Some animals use song and dance in their courtship displays. Red deer stags roar to warn rival males to keep away. A male scorpion holds the female's pincers and walks round her in a type of dance. A male stickleback fish performs a zig-zag dance to attract a female to his nest. She lays eggs which he then guards.

Amazing FACT

Naked mole rats are rodents that live in family groups in underground burrows. Because they live in darkness, their eyesight is very poor. When they want to find a mate, therefore, males bang their heads against the roofs of their tunnels. The females pick up the vibrations.

A naked mole rat.

A red deer stag's magnificent antlers are a sign of its age, size and strength. In fights with rivals, males roar and lock antlers, risking serious injury.

THE JUMPING SPIDER DANCE

Shining colours on front legs attract female.

For male spiders, mating is a risky business. If they are not careful, females may mistake them for prey and eat them. Males have different ways of identifying themselves. Jumping spiders make signals with their legs to show females that they are ready to mate.

Male birds have many ways of attracting a female for breeding. They sing, dance, show off their fine feathers and colours, bring gifts or display their building skills.

FABULOUS FEATHERS

Male birds of paradise have fabulous feathers which they use in courtship. A Count Raggi's bird of paradise (see right) has long, red plumes on his back. He hangs upside-down in a tree and fans out his feathers in a dazzling display to impress a mate.

A male peacock fans out his magnificent tail feathers and shakes them at the drab, brown female. The brighter his feathers, the more likely he is to find a mate.

To attract a mate, a male frigatebird blows up the large, red pouch on his throat. He may keep the pouch inflated for hours waiting for a female to choose him.

As many as ten Count Raggi's birds of paradise display in one tree. Females choose the bird with the most beautiful plumage.

BUSY BUILDERS

The male satin bowerbird works hard to impress a mate. He builds a 'bower' or arch from two rows of twigs, which he then decorates with blue objects, such as flowers, feathers and shells. He even paints the bower with blueberry juice.

A female bowerbird inspects the male's handiwork. If she likes what she sees, she will stay and mate with him.

A sage grouse displaying.

Amazing FACT

At breeding time, many species of grouse gather at big sites, called leks. Each male has its own patch where it struts about and fans out its feathers. Hundreds of grouse display together. The females watch the display to choose a mate.

Sign language

• Scientists have not been able to teach chimpanzees or gorillas to speak, but they have trained them to use sign language. A gorilla called Koko knew about 1000 different words.

Alligator bellows

• Alligators are very noisy reptiles. American alligators bellow to attract a mate for breeding. Their call sounds like a lion roaring and can be heard 150 metres away.

Deaf as a snake

• All snakes are deaf to sounds carried by the air. Their bodies pick up vibrations on the ground.

Loudest insect

• The male cicada is the loudest insect. Its song can be heard over 400 metres away. Cicadas use their songs to attract females.

Go electric

• The duck-billed platypus finds its food underwater. But it seals its eyes and ears so it cannot see or hear. It locates tiny animals with its beak by picking up electricity made by their twitching muscles.

Sharpest hearing

• Barn owls probably have the best hearing of any type of bird. They use it to catch live prey in the dark

Loudest voices

• Blue whales and fin whales have the loudest voices of any animals. When they are communicating, their songs can be heard almost 1000 kilometres away.

Brainy bird

• A budgerigar from Britain was able to say words in English, Russian, Spanish, German, Welsh and Icelandic.

GLOSSARY

antennae
Feelers on an animal's head which help it to touch and sense things, and to detect tastes and smells.

bacteria
Tiny living things which live inside animals. Some do useful jobs and are harmless; others cause disease.

courtship
The way in which animals use displays to attract a mate.

glands
Parts of an animal's body which produce special substances.

luminous
Shining or glowing in the dark.

migrating
Birds' yearly, long-distance journeys between their breeding and feeding grounds.

mimic
Another word for copy or imitate.

navigation
Finding the way.

nocturnal
Animals that rest during the day and are active at night.

organs
Parts of an animal's body which have special jobs to do.

pigment
Another word for colour.

predators
Animals that hunt and kill other animals, called prey, for food.

roosting
Sleeping or resting.

species
A group of living things that are grouped together because they have similar features.

territory
An area or patch of land which gives animals food and safety.